PRINCEWILL LAGANG

Courtship Conversations: Building a Strong Foundation

First published by PRINCEWILL LAGANG 2023

Copyright © 2023 by Princewill Lagang

All rights reserved. No part of this publication may be reproduced, stored or transmitted in any form or by any means, electronic, mechanical, photocopying, recording, scanning, or otherwise without written permission from the publisher. It is illegal to copy this book, post it to a website, or distribute it by any other means without permission.

Princewill Lagang asserts the moral right to be identified as the author of this work.

First edition

This book was professionally typeset on Reedsy.
Find out more at reedsy.com

# Contents

| | | |
|---|---|---|
| 1 | Courtship Conversations - Building a Strong Foundation | 1 |
| 2 | The Early Stages of Courtship | 4 |
| 3 | Trust and Intimacy in Courtship | 7 |
| 4 | Navigating Life's Challenges Together | 10 |
| 5 | Keeping the Flame Alive - Nurturing Passion and Romance | 13 |
| 6 | Preparing for Long-Term Commitment | 17 |
| 7 | Securing the Foundation - A Love That Stands the Test of... | 21 |
| 8 | Taking the Next Step - From Courtship to Lifelong Love | 25 |
| 9 | A Joyful Union - The Wedding and Beyond | 29 |
| 10 | Sustaining a Fulfilling Partnership - The Joys and... | 33 |
| 11 | The Wisdom of a Long-Lasting Marriage | 36 |
| 12 | A Legacy of Enduring Love | 40 |
| 13 | Chapter 13 | 45 |

# 1

# Courtship Conversations - Building a Strong Foundation

The sun dipped below the horizon, casting a warm, golden glow across the park. Couples strolled hand in hand, their laughter filling the air, as if love had become the natural rhythm of the evening. Among them, Sarah and John walked with a sense of anticipation and excitement. It was the beginning of their journey together, a journey that would take them through the intricate art of courtship, as they embarked on the adventure of building a strong foundation for their relationship.

The Prelude

Sarah and John had met through a mutual friend at a cozy café in their small town. Their connection was immediate, sparking an undeniable chemistry that lingered long after they had parted ways. As they exchanged numbers that fateful afternoon, they knew that this was the start of something special, something worth nurturing and cherishing.

Little did they know, their path to lasting love and happiness would be paved with meaningful conversations, shared experiences, and a deep understanding of one another. The courtship period, often overlooked in our fast-paced world, is a crucial phase of any budding relationship. It's a time to explore, connect, and build a strong foundation that can weather the inevitable storms of life.

Navigating Modern Love

The modern world has brought about many changes in the way people approach love and relationships. Fast-paced lives, technology, and a constant rush to the future have left many feeling disconnected from the simple yet profound act of forming a deep, lasting connection with another person. In an era of swiping right and instant gratification, the concept of courtship may seem old-fashioned, but it is, in fact, more relevant than ever.

This chapter seeks to explore the beauty of courtship in the modern age, providing a roadmap for building a strong foundation in any romantic relationship. It emphasizes the importance of deep, meaningful conversations, as they are the pillars upon which a lasting love can be built.

The Power of Conversations

In the digital age, communication has never been easier. Texts, emails, and social media platforms allow us to stay connected with one another, yet true conversations are often relegated to the background. The art of meaningful conversation is what distinguishes a courtship from mere dating. It is a bridge that connects two hearts, a tool for discovering each other's dreams, fears, and desires, and a platform for building a strong emotional foundation.

This chapter will delve into the significance of open, honest, and heartfelt conversations. It will teach you how to ask the right questions, listen actively, and create an environment where both you and your partner feel safe and valued. Through these conversations, you will not only discover who your partner is but also who you can become together.

## The Road Ahead

As Sarah and John continued their leisurely walk in the park, their conversations flowed seamlessly. They shared their dreams, their pasts, and their vulnerabilities. With each word exchanged, their connection grew stronger, and the foundation of their budding relationship became more solid.

In the chapters that follow, we will explore the various dimensions of courtship conversations. You'll learn how to navigate the early stages of courtship, address challenging topics, and deepen your emotional connection. Building a strong foundation in your relationship requires effort, commitment, and a willingness to communicate openly and honestly.

So, join us on this journey through the art of courtship conversations, and discover the magic of building a love that will stand the test of time.

# 2

# The Early Stages of Courtship

As Sarah and John's relationship blossomed, they found themselves at the heart of their courtship, the early stages where the foundation for their love story would be laid. This chapter delves into the crucial moments, the defining conversations, and the milestones that shape the path to a strong foundation in a courtship.

Setting the Stage

In the early stages of courtship, there's a palpable excitement in the air. Everything feels fresh and full of potential. As you embark on this journey, remember that the first impression you create and the conversations you engage in will set the tone for the entire relationship. It's an exhilarating, often nerve-wracking time, but it's also an opportunity to explore and connect.

The First Date

The first date is often a mixture of nervousness and anticipation. It's your opportunity to learn more about your potential partner and to leave a lasting impression. Engage in conversation that shows genuine interest in their life, passions, and aspirations. Remember, it's not just about what you say but how you say it—maintain good eye contact, listen actively, and be yourself.

## Getting to Know Each Other

Once the first date hurdle is crossed, it's time to delve deeper. Share stories from your past, talk about your families, and discuss your dreams for the future. The key is to build a sense of familiarity and trust. Ask open-ended questions that invite your partner to share, and be prepared to reciprocate.

## The Art of Communication

### Honesty and Authenticity

Open, honest communication is the cornerstone of any successful courtship. It's a time to be yourself, to share your true thoughts and feelings. This authenticity is the glue that holds a relationship together. As Sarah and John discovered, it's in vulnerability that true connections are formed.

### Respectful Boundaries

While open communication is essential, it's equally important to be mindful of each other's boundaries. Some topics may be too personal or sensitive to discuss early on. Understand and respect your partner's comfort level, and be patient. The process of courtship is a journey, not a destination.

## Navigating Challenges

### Conflict Resolution

The early stages of courtship can be a testing ground for how you handle conflicts and disagreements. It's essential to approach these situations with empathy, respect, and a desire to find common ground. Learning to navigate conflicts with grace can set a strong foundation for your relationship.

### Dealing with Baggage

As conversations get deeper, past relationships, traumas, and personal struggles may come to light. It's important to approach these topics with empathy and support. Listen without judgment and provide the emotional space your partner needs to heal and grow.

## Creating Shared Experiences

### Building Memories

Shared experiences play a vital role in courtship. They create memories that bond you and provide a backdrop for conversations. Whether it's a romantic getaway, a fun outing, or even just cooking dinner together, these experiences foster connection.

### Goals and Future Planning

In the early stages, it's beneficial to discuss your goals and future plans. Are your long-term aspirations aligned? Talking about where you see yourselves in a few years can help ensure you're on the same page and working toward a shared future.

### Looking Forward

As Sarah and John continued their courtship journey, they were laying a strong foundation through their conversations and shared experiences. In the chapters ahead, we will explore deeper and more nuanced aspects of courtship, addressing issues such as trust, intimacy, and long-term commitment. Building a strong foundation in your relationship is a journey, and the early stages set the tone for what's to come. Remember, these moments of discovery and connection are the building blocks of a lasting love story.

# 3

# Trust and Intimacy in Courtship

In the intricate dance of courtship, as Sarah and John continued their journey, they began to realize the profound role trust and intimacy play in building a strong foundation. This chapter explores how these two essential elements shape a blossoming relationship.

Trust: The Cornerstone of Connection

Trust in Communication

Open and honest communication forms the bedrock of trust in a courtship. It's about being reliable, sharing your thoughts, and being receptive to your partner's feelings and ideas. As Sarah and John discovered, trust flourishes when you feel safe expressing yourself without fear of judgment or betrayal.

Building Consistency

Reliability and consistency are vital in fostering trust. Keeping your promises, showing up when you say you will, and following through on commitments all contribute to the growth of trust in a relationship. Trust is not just about words but also about actions.

### Past Baggage and Trust Issues

Addressing past trust issues is crucial in the early stages of courtship. If either partner has experienced betrayal or heartbreak in previous relationships, open conversations can help heal old wounds and create a foundation of trust in the new relationship. Listening and understanding each other's fears and insecurities is a powerful step in building trust.

## Intimacy: The Art of Connection

### Emotional Intimacy

True intimacy is more than just physical closeness; it's about emotional connection. Share your feelings, fears, and joys openly. In courtship, it's essential to create a safe space where both partners can be vulnerable and authentic. Intimacy begins when you let your guard down and invite your partner into the deeper recesses of your heart.

### Physical Intimacy

Physical intimacy, while important, should be approached with care and consideration. In the early stages of courtship, it's crucial to communicate your boundaries and ensure you both feel comfortable and respected. Consent and open dialogue are fundamental in creating a healthy physical connection.

### Cultivating Intellectual Intimacy

Beyond emotions and the physical realm, intellectual intimacy is about sharing ideas and perspectives. Engaging in stimulating conversations, discussing shared interests, and learning from one another create a bond that transcends the superficial.

## Challenges in Trust and Intimacy

### Fear and Vulnerability

Fear can be a significant barrier to both trust and intimacy. Fear of rejection, abandonment, or not being good enough can hinder the depth of connection in courtship. Acknowledge these fears, communicate about them, and provide reassurance to your partner as you navigate these challenges together.

### Managing Differences

In courtship, you'll inevitably encounter differences in values, beliefs, and expectations. These can be opportunities for growth and understanding. Approach these conversations with respect and curiosity, and seek to find common ground or compromise when necessary.

### Looking Ahead

As Sarah and John continued their courtship, they realized that building a strong foundation wasn't just about surface-level attractions. Trust and intimacy were the building blocks upon which lasting love was constructed. In the chapters to come, we will explore topics like long-term commitment, navigating life's challenges together, and maintaining the flame of passion. Trust and intimacy are not destinations but ongoing journeys, continuously evolving as your relationship deepens. With patience, communication, and a willingness to open your heart, you can nurture these essential elements and create a love story that stands the test of time.

# 4

# Navigating Life's Challenges Together

As Sarah and John's courtship journey progressed, they encountered new challenges and opportunities that tested the strength of their bond. This chapter explores how couples can navigate life's challenges together while continuing to build a strong foundation for their relationship.

Facing Life's Curveballs

Life is unpredictable, and it often throws unexpected challenges our way. In courtship, it's important to acknowledge that you and your partner will face both individual and shared difficulties. The way you handle these challenges can significantly impact the foundation of your relationship.

Supporting Each Other

During times of crisis or difficulty, it's essential to be a source of support for one another. Listen actively, empathize, and offer encouragement. Sharing your partner's burdens fosters a sense of security and trust in the relationship.

Maintaining Independence

While supporting each other is crucial, it's also important to maintain individuality and independence. Your own well-being and personal growth should not be sacrificed for the sake of the relationship. Encourage your partner to pursue their passions and self-care, and ensure that you do the same.

Money Matters

Finances can be a significant source of stress in any relationship. In courtship, discussing money can help you gain insight into each other's values and financial habits. This chapter explores how to approach financial conversations and work together to manage financial challenges.

Open and Honest Financial Conversations

Discussing finances openly, without judgment, is key to financial harmony. Share your financial goals, debt, and spending habits. Creating a joint budget can help you both understand how you'll manage finances as a couple.

Financial Problem-Solving

When faced with financial challenges, approach them as a team. Find solutions together, make joint decisions, and adapt as needed. It's a chance to showcase your ability to work together and find common ground.

Balancing Friendships and Relationships

Maintaining a healthy balance between your social life and your relationship can be challenging in courtship. This chapter explores the importance of nurturing your social connections while also prioritizing your partner.

Setting Boundaries

Clearly communicate your expectations and boundaries regarding social interactions with friends. Ensure that both you and your partner have time for personal and shared experiences.

Career Ambitions and Long-Term Goals

In courtship, it's essential to discuss career ambitions and long-term goals. This can help you understand each other's aspirations and build a foundation that supports your individual growth and shared future.

Supporting Each Other's Goals

Encourage your partner in their career aspirations, and seek ways to align your goals where possible. Discuss how you envision your future together and work on a plan that accommodates both of your ambitions.

Looking Forward

Navigating life's challenges together is a pivotal aspect of building a strong foundation in your courtship. As Sarah and John continued their journey, they realized that by facing these challenges with open communication, support, and understanding, their bond grew stronger.

In the upcoming chapters, we will explore topics such as maintaining passion and romance in your relationship, deepening your emotional connection, and preparing for long-term commitment. Your courtship is a journey of growth and discovery, and each challenge you overcome brings you closer to a love story that will stand the test of time.

# 5

# Keeping the Flame Alive - Nurturing Passion and Romance

As Sarah and John's courtship journey continued to evolve, they recognized the importance of nurturing passion and romance in their relationship. In this chapter, we will explore how couples can keep the flame of love burning brightly while building a strong foundation.

The Importance of Passion

Passion is the driving force behind any successful courtship. It's the spark that ignites your connection, keeps your relationship exciting, and deepens your bond. Without passion, a courtship can grow stale. Here's how to maintain that fiery connection:

Physical Intimacy

Physical intimacy is a powerful way to fuel passion. Regular affection, romantic gestures, and an active sex life can keep the connection alive and thriving. Don't shy away from discussing your desires, needs, and fantasies with your partner.

## Spontaneity and Surprise

Surprise your partner with spontaneous acts of love and thoughtfulness. Plan date nights, leave love notes, or whisk them away on a surprise weekend getaway. These gestures remind your partner of your love and keep the courtship exciting.

## Cultivating Romance

Romance adds a layer of depth to your courtship, fostering emotional intimacy and making your relationship more meaningful. It's about creating cherished memories together and showing your partner how much they mean to you:

## Date Nights

Make date nights a regular occurrence in your courtship. These dedicated times for just the two of you keep the romance alive. Try new experiences, revisit favorite places, or simply enjoy a cozy night in with a home-cooked meal.

## Shared Interests

Pursuing shared interests can be a great way to bond and reignite your passion. Explore hobbies, activities, or creative ventures together. It's an opportunity to grow and connect on a deeper level.

## Maintaining Emotional Connection

Emotional intimacy is the bedrock of a strong relationship. Your courtship conversations should continue to deepen this connection, ensuring your love stands the test of time:

## Vulnerability and Communication

Continue to be open and honest with each other. Share your fears, hopes, and dreams. Create a space where you both feel safe being vulnerable. Effective communication is the key to maintaining emotional connection.

## Regular Check-Ins

In the hustle and bustle of life, it's easy to neglect each other's emotional needs. Make a habit of regular check-ins. Ask your partner how they're feeling, what they need, and how you can support them. These conversations can strengthen your bond.

## Managing Differences

Throughout your courtship, you'll discover differences in opinions, interests, and expectations. Handling these differences with grace is key to maintaining a strong foundation:

## Compromise and Understanding

Learn the art of compromise. It's about finding common ground, respecting each other's perspectives, and accommodating each other's needs. Understand that differences can be opportunities for growth and learning.

## Looking Forward

As Sarah and John continued their journey, they realized that keeping the flame of passion and romance alive was a continuous effort. The spark that ignited their courtship needed nurturing to grow into a strong, enduring love.

In the upcoming chapters, we will delve into the preparation for long-term commitment, managing life's transitions together, and securing the foundation of a relationship that will stand the test of time. Nurturing passion and romance is an ongoing process, and with dedication and heartfelt conversations, your love story can continue to flourish.

# 6

# Preparing for Long-Term Commitment

As Sarah and John's courtship journey progressed, they began to contemplate the possibility of a long-term commitment. In this chapter, we explore the conversations and considerations that arise when preparing for such a commitment and how it further strengthens the foundation of their relationship.

The Decision to Commit

Long-term commitment is a significant milestone in a courtship. It signifies the intention to build a life together. This chapter addresses the steps and conversations involved in preparing for commitment.

Assessing Compatibility

Before taking the step toward commitment, it's crucial to evaluate your compatibility as a couple. Ask yourselves fundamental questions:

- Do you share similar values, life goals, and long-term visions?
   - Are you emotionally and financially prepared for the responsibilities that come with commitment?
   - Have you discussed the possibility of marriage or cohabitation?

- Are there any unresolved issues or concerns that need addressing?

These questions serve as a foundation for the conversations you'll have in preparing for a long-term commitment.

The Importance of Communication

Open and honest communication remains a cornerstone of courtship, particularly as you approach a more committed phase in your relationship.

Discussing Expectations

Share your expectations and desires regarding the commitment. This includes your thoughts on marriage, cohabitation, financial arrangements, and long-term goals. These conversations help align your visions for the future.

Navigating Family and Friends

Discuss how your commitment will impact your relationships with family and friends. Are there cultural or religious expectations to consider? Ensure that both partners feel supported and comfortable with the influence of their respective social circles.

Planning for the Future

As you prepare for a long-term commitment, it's essential to discuss the practical aspects of your future together.

Financial Planning

Create a financial plan that outlines how you'll manage your finances together. This may include joint bank accounts, budgeting, and financial goals. Transparency about money matters is key to a successful long-term commitment.

## Living Arrangements

If you haven't already, discuss your living arrangements. Decide whether you'll move in together, purchase a home, or continue living separately. Address any logistical considerations, such as location, space, and lifestyle preferences.

## Preparing for Challenges

Long-term commitment comes with its own set of challenges, and it's essential to address potential issues proactively.

## Conflict Resolution

Discuss how you'll handle conflicts and disagreements as a committed couple. Establish ground rules for effective communication and problem-solving.

## Maintaining Individuality

Emphasize the importance of maintaining individuality and personal growth within the relationship. Commitment should enhance your lives, not limit your individual aspirations.

## Looking Forward

As Sarah and John navigated the waters of preparing for long-term commitment, they recognized that building a strong foundation was an ongoing journey. Their conversations had paved the way for a deeper, more meaningful connection.

In the chapters to come, we will explore topics like managing life's transitions together and securing the foundation of a relationship that will stand the test of time. Long-term commitment is a significant step in a courtship, but it's only the beginning of a lifetime of growth and love.

# 7

# Securing the Foundation - A Love That Stands the Test of Time

As Sarah and John's courtship journey reached a significant milestone with their long-term commitment, they continued to strengthen the foundation of their relationship. In this chapter, we explore how couples can secure the foundation of their love, making it resilient in the face of life's challenges.

Preparing for Life's Transitions

Life is a series of transitions, and how you navigate these changes together can significantly impact your relationship. This chapter discusses how to prepare for and embrace transitions in your courtship.

Communication during Change

Transitions, whether they involve career shifts, moving, or personal growth, require effective communication. Be open about your feelings, expectations, and concerns. Support each other during these transitions, acknowledging that change can be challenging.

### Adapting to New Roles

As your relationship evolves, you may take on new roles or responsibilities. Discuss how you will adapt to these changes and continue to share the load. Remember to maintain a sense of equality and mutual respect.

### Maintaining Emotional Connection

Emotional intimacy remains a crucial aspect of your courtship, and even as your relationship deepens, it requires nurturing.

### Regular Check-Ins

Keep the habit of regular check-ins alive. Ask your partner how they're feeling, what they need, and how you can support them. These conversations maintain the emotional connection and reinforce your commitment to each other.

### Rekindling Romance

Romance shouldn't wane with time. Continue to plan date nights and special moments that reignite the passion in your relationship. Regularly expressing your love and appreciation keeps the flame alive.

### Weathering Life's Storms

No relationship is without its challenges. As you secure the foundation of your love, it's crucial to be prepared for and resilient in the face of life's storms.

### Supporting Each Other

During difficult times, be a source of support for your partner. Show empathy, actively listen, and offer encouragement. Remember that the storms of life are more manageable when faced as a team.

Maintaining Trust

Trust is tested in challenging moments. Keep communication open, be transparent about your feelings, and navigate these situations with honesty and empathy. Building trust during adversity can deepen your connection.

Planning for the Future

As you secure the foundation of your relationship, you'll continue to make plans for your shared future.

Setting Goals

Regularly revisit your goals as a couple. Discuss your plans for the long-term, and make adjustments as needed. Setting new goals together keeps your relationship vibrant and purposeful.

Preparation for a Lifetime

As you look ahead, consider how your commitment will withstand the test of time. Discuss matters like estate planning, creating a will, and long-term healthcare. These discussions can bring peace of mind and strengthen your bond.

Reflecting on Your Journey

As Sarah and John reflected on their journey and the strength of their foundation, they understood that a successful courtship is an ongoing process. Building a love that stands the test of time requires commitment, effort, and the willingness to adapt as life unfolds.

In the chapters to come, we will explore the final stages of courtship and what it means to take your relationship to the next level. Your love story, secured by a strong foundation, is a testament to your shared growth, resilience, and enduring love.

# 8

# Taking the Next Step - From Courtship to Lifelong Love

As Sarah and John's courtship journey reached its culmination, they found themselves ready to transition to the next stage of their relationship—a lifelong commitment. This chapter explores the essential conversations and considerations that come into play as couples take the final step from courtship to building a love meant to last a lifetime.

The Road to Lifelong Love

The journey from courtship to lifelong love is an exciting and significant one. It signifies a profound commitment to building a life together, facing both joys and challenges as a united team.

The Importance of Reflecting

Before taking this step, it's crucial to reflect on your courtship journey. What have you learned about yourselves and each other? How have you grown individually and as a couple? Reflecting on your experiences can help you better understand your readiness for the next level of commitment.

## The Proposal and Engagement

The proposal is often a highlight in the transition from courtship to lifelong love. It's a moment that symbolizes your commitment to each other and your shared future.

### Choosing the Right Time and Place

Consider the timing and setting for your proposal. It should be a moment that is meaningful for both of you and aligns with your values and preferences.

### Planning the Engagement

After the proposal, engagement is a period of planning and preparation for your lifelong commitment. It involves decisions such as the wedding, where you'll live, and what your life together will look like.

## Legal and Financial Aspects

With a lifelong commitment come legal and financial considerations that ensure your mutual well-being.

### Legal Arrangements

Discuss matters like prenuptial agreements, wills, and legal responsibilities. These conversations are essential for your peace of mind and for ensuring your financial and legal interests are protected.

### Financial Planning

Continue to refine your financial planning and budgeting as you prepare for a lifetime together. Discuss how you'll manage your finances, save for the future, and navigate any financial challenges that arise.

## Building a Supportive Network

As you transition to lifelong love, consider the support system you'll have in place.

### Supportive Friends and Family

Discuss how your friends and family will continue to play a role in your lives. This may involve decisions about holiday celebrations, family events, and social connections.

## Preparing for Marriage

If marriage is part of your lifelong commitment, thorough preparation is essential.

### Pre-Marital Counseling

Consider pre-marital counseling as a way to strengthen your relationship and prepare for the unique challenges of marriage. A qualified counselor can guide you through discussions on communication, conflict resolution, and roles and responsibilities.

## Looking Forward

Transitioning from courtship to lifelong love is a profound step in your relationship journey. The foundation you've built through communication, trust, and shared experiences is now a sturdy base upon which you'll construct your life together.

In the upcoming chapters, we will explore the final steps of your journey toward lifelong love, including the wedding, adjusting to married life, and maintaining a happy and fulfilling marriage. Your transition to lifelong love is the culmination of your dedication, and it paves the way for a rich and enduring love story.

# 9

# A Joyful Union - The Wedding and Beyond

As Sarah and John's journey progressed from courtship to the threshold of marriage, this chapter explores the vital conversations, preparations, and considerations that come into play as couples plan their wedding and take the first steps into married life.

The Wedding: A Celebration of Love

The wedding marks the official transition from courtship to marriage. It's a celebration of love, commitment, and the promise of a life shared together.

Defining the Wedding

Decide the style, size, and location of your wedding. Whether it's an intimate ceremony or a grand celebration, make sure it aligns with your vision as a couple.

Setting a Date

Choosing a date is an exciting and important step. It should be a date that holds significance for you both, aligning with your courtship journey and future aspirations.

Guest List and Invitations

Determine who will be part of your celebration and prepare your guest list. Create and send invitations, and plan the logistics of the event.

Marriage Preparation

Preparing for marriage is a significant part of the transition. It involves several important aspects that will shape your life together.

Pre-Marital Counseling

Engage in pre-marital counseling to strengthen your relationship. A counselor can help you navigate essential conversations, provide tools for conflict resolution, and enhance your understanding of the challenges and joys of marriage.

Legal and Financial Aspects

Address legal matters, including obtaining a marriage license. Review financial responsibilities and discuss how you'll manage finances as a married couple.

Transitioning to Married Life

The initial stages of married life can be a period of adjustment as you settle into your new roles and responsibilities.

Communication in Marriage

Continue the open and honest communication that has been the foundation of your relationship. Discuss your expectations, roles, and responsibilities as a married couple.

Building a Shared Life

As you transition to married life, you'll face decisions about living arrangements, joint finances, and shared goals. Embrace this journey as you build a life that aligns with your vision as a couple.

Nurturing Your Love

Just as in courtship, nurturing your love remains essential in marriage.

Date Nights and Romance

Keep the romance alive with regular date nights and special moments that remind you of the love and passion that brought you together.

Emotional Connection

Maintain your emotional connection by continuing to have meaningful conversations, being open to vulnerability, and offering each other support and love.

Looking Forward

The transition from courtship to marriage is a significant step in your journey as a couple. The foundation you've built throughout your courtship journey has prepared you for a lifetime of love and growth together.

In the upcoming chapters, we will explore the ongoing joys and challenges of marriage, including navigating the everyday, building a family, and sustaining a happy and fulfilling partnership. Your journey is a testament to your commitment and dedication to building a strong and lasting love story.

# 10

# Sustaining a Fulfilling Partnership - The Joys and Challenges of Marriage

As Sarah and John's journey from courtship to marriage unfolded, they encountered the many facets of married life. In this chapter, we explore the vital conversations, considerations, and actions that come into play as couples sustain a fulfilling partnership through the joys and challenges of marriage.

Everyday Life as a Couple

Marriage is a journey of shared experiences and mutual growth. Embracing the everyday aspects of life as a couple is fundamental to building a strong, lasting partnership.

Effective Communication

Continue the open and honest communication that has been a cornerstone of your relationship. Be attentive, express your thoughts and feelings, and actively listen to your partner.

Quality Time Together

Make an effort to spend quality time together. Date nights, shared hobbies, or simple evenings in can help maintain the emotional connection that brought you together.

Navigating Challenges

Every marriage faces its share of challenges. How you address and overcome them can significantly impact your partnership.

Conflict Resolution

Develop effective conflict resolution skills. Learn to argue constructively, compromise, and find common ground when disagreements arise.

Financial Management

As a married couple, financial planning is even more crucial. Regularly review your financial goals, budget, and ensure you're both on the same page regarding money management.

Building a Family

For many couples, building a family is a natural progression. This stage requires thoughtful consideration and preparation.

Family Planning

Discuss your family planning goals, including the timing of having children, and how you will handle important parenting decisions.

Supporting Each Other as Parents

As parents, support each other in your respective roles. Share parenting responsibilities, offer emotional support, and communicate about the challenges and joys of raising a family.

Maintaining Intimacy

Maintaining physical and emotional intimacy is essential for a fulfilling partnership.

Intimate Connection

Continue to nurture your physical connection. Keep the spark alive through physical affection and open communication about your desires and needs.

Emotional Bond

Foster your emotional connection. Engage in conversations that deepen your understanding of each other's evolving hopes, dreams, and fears.

Looking Forward

Marriage is a journey of love, growth, and partnership. The foundation you've built through courtship and the transitions you've navigated have prepared you for a life of fulfillment together.

In the final chapters of this book, we will explore the enduring aspects of a lifelong commitment, including the wisdom of a long-lasting marriage, facing the tests of time, and cherishing the enduring love that is your legacy. Your marriage journey is a testament to your dedication and your ability to build a strong and lasting love story.

# 11

# The Wisdom of a Long-Lasting Marriage

As Sarah and John's journey from courtship to marriage unfolded over the years, they amassed invaluable experience and wisdom. In this chapter, we explore the enduring aspects of a lifelong commitment, delving into the wisdom of a long-lasting marriage that has weathered the tests of time.

Embracing the Passage of Time

In a marriage that has stood the test of time, the passage of years is a source of wisdom, growth, and reflection.

Continued Communication

Marriages that endure are characterized by ongoing, meaningful communication. Couples who have been together for a long time have learned to listen, express themselves, and adapt to changing circumstances.

Patience and Understanding

The wisdom of a long-lasting marriage is built upon patience and understanding. Partners grow, change, and face challenges, but they do so with a commitment to supporting and accepting each other.

### Shared Memories and Experiences

A marriage that has stood the test of time is filled with shared memories and experiences.

### Cherishing Milestones

Couples who have been together for many years cherish the milestones they've achieved together. These milestones often become symbols of their enduring love.

### Facing Challenges Together

Every marriage faces its share of challenges. Those that last are built on the ability to face adversity as a team, learning from each challenge and emerging stronger.

### The Art of Compromise

Long-lasting marriages are often characterized by the art of compromise.

### Balancing Independence

Couples who have been together for years understand the importance of maintaining their individuality while supporting each other's growth and aspirations.

### Seeking Common Ground

In long-lasting marriages, compromise is a way of life. Couples learn to find common ground and make joint decisions that benefit their partnership.

## Staying Connected

The wisdom of a long-lasting marriage is rooted in maintaining a deep emotional and physical connection.

## Nurturing Intimacy

Physical intimacy continues to be a vital component of a long-lasting marriage. Partners prioritize nurturing their physical connection, keeping the spark alive throughout the years.

## Support and Encouragement

The enduring love of a long-lasting marriage is built on a foundation of unwavering support and encouragement. Partners uplift each other in pursuit of their dreams and endeavors.

## Passing Down Wisdom

Long-lasting marriages often involve the passing down of wisdom to the next generation.

## Modeling Love and Commitment

Couples who have been together for a long time become models of love and commitment for their children and grandchildren, passing on their wisdom through their actions and advice.

## Looking Forward

The wisdom of a long-lasting marriage is a testament to the enduring love, growth, and commitment of a couple. Sarah and John, like many others, have built a strong foundation for their love story through their dedication to each other and their shared experiences.

In the final chapter of this book, we will explore the legacy of enduring love, the value of cherishing your relationship, and the journey of love that lasts a lifetime. Your story is a living example of the wisdom and commitment that defines a long-lasting marriage.

# 12

# A Legacy of Enduring Love

As Sarah and John's love story continued to evolve, they found themselves at a stage where their relationship had stood the test of time. In this final chapter, we explore the value of cherishing your relationship and the journey of love that lasts a lifetime, leaving behind a legacy of enduring love.

Cherishing Your Relationship

A love story that endures through the years is one worth cherishing. As Sarah and John found, this stage of a relationship is an opportunity to reflect on the significance of your connection.

Gratitude and Appreciation

Take the time to express your gratitude and appreciation for your partner. Reflect on the moments, challenges, and joys you've shared and how they've shaped your life.

Rekindling Romance

Rekindle the romance in your relationship by continuing to plan special moments and keeping the passion alive. Find new ways to connect and express your love.

The Value of Endurance

Enduring love is a testament to your commitment and the strength of your partnership.

Weathering Life's Storms

Reflect on the storms you've weathered together and how you've come out stronger. These experiences have deepened your connection and fortified your love.

Life's Milestones

Celebrate the milestones you've achieved together, from personal accomplishments to family growth. These moments are the building blocks of your enduring love.

Passing on Wisdom

A love that stands the test of time is often a source of wisdom and inspiration for others.

Supporting Future Generations

Share your experiences and wisdom with the next generation. Support your children and grandchildren in their own journeys of love, offering advice and guidance based on your enduring love story.

Embracing a Lifetime of Love

The journey of love that lasts a lifetime is a remarkable one, and it's a legacy that endures beyond your years together.

Living Your Love Story

Embrace the concept of living your love story every day. Continue to nurture your emotional and physical connection, make memories, and find joy in each other's company.

The Enduring Legacy

Your love story will leave an enduring legacy, inspiring others and serving as a testament to the power of commitment, communication, and a strong foundation.

The Final Chapter

As Sarah and John reflected on their enduring love, they understood that the strength of their connection was a testament to the commitment they had to each other and the dedication they put into building a strong foundation.

Your love story is unique, and it will leave a legacy for those who come after you. As you navigate the years together, cherish the moments, continue to build on your foundation, and leave behind a story of enduring love that will inspire and uplift others.

Title: Courtship Conversations: Building a Strong Foundation

Book Summary:

"Courtship Conversations: Building a Strong Foundation" is a comprehensive guide that traces the journey of Sarah and John, a fictional couple, as they navigate the intricate path of courtship and marriage. This book is a testament to the power of communication, trust, and understanding in building a lasting love story. It is divided into twelve chapters, each focusing on a different aspect of building a strong foundation for a successful relationship.

In the early chapters, the book delves into the importance of open and honest communication, emphasizing the need for couples to express their thoughts, emotions, and desires. It highlights the significance of creating a safe space for vulnerability and authenticity, where trust can thrive.

As the story of Sarah and John unfolds, readers are introduced to the challenges and joys of courtship. The book addresses the need to navigate past baggage and insecurities, and it stresses the importance of addressing trust issues and fears from previous relationships.

The subsequent chapters explore the essential elements of courtship, including trust and intimacy. Building consistency, reliability, and understanding are key components of trust, while emotional, physical, and intellectual intimacy are the building blocks of a deep connection between partners.

Throughout the book, the authors highlight the challenges that couples face and offer guidance on managing differences, fears, and insecurities. It also provides valuable insights into preparing for long-term commitment, discussing legal and financial aspects, and understanding the implications of marriage.

The later chapters delve into the ongoing journey of love, where couples are encouraged to nurture the flame of passion and keep the romance alive. The importance of maintaining emotional intimacy, understanding each other's desires, and navigating life's transitions together are emphasized.

As the book nears its conclusion, it focuses on the wisdom of a long-lasting marriage and the importance of passing on the legacy of enduring love. It encourages couples to cherish their relationship and inspire the next generation with their enduring commitment.

"Courtship Conversations: Building a Strong Foundation" is a guidebook that takes readers on a journey from the early stages of courtship to the enduring legacy of an enduring love. It offers practical advice, real-life scenarios, and valuable insights into creating a strong foundation for a lasting, fulfilling relationship. Whether you're embarking on a new relationship or seeking to strengthen an existing one, this book provides a roadmap to building a love story that stands the test of time.

13

# Chapter 13

www.ingramcontent.com/pod-product-compliance
Lightning Source LLC
LaVergne TN
LVHW012130070526
838202LV00056B/5937